Dulce

SERIES EDITORS

Chris Abani

John Alba Cutler

Reginald Gibbons

Susannah Young-ah Gottlieb

Ed Roberson

Matthew Shenoda

Dulce

Poems

Marcelo Hernandez Castillo

NORTHWESTERN UNIVERSITY PRESS

EVANSTON, ILLINOIS

Northwestern University Press
www.nupress.northwestern.edu

Northwestern University Poetry and Poetics Colloquium
www.poetry.northwestern.edu

Printed in the United States of America

10 9 8 7 6 5 4 3 2 1

Library of Congress Cataloging-in-Publication Data

Names: Hernandez Castillo, Marcelo, 1988– author.
Title: Dulce : poems / Marcelo Hernandez Castillo.
Other titles: Drinking gourd chapbook poetry prize.
Description: Evanston, Illinois : Northwestern University Press, 2018. |
Series: Drinking gourd chapbook poetry prize
Identifiers: LCCN 2017038965 | ISBN 9780810136960 (pbk. : alk. paper)
Classification: LCC PS3608.E76845 D85 2018 | DDC 811.6—dc23
LC record available at https://lccn.loc.gov/2017038965

For Rubi

For Antonia

Sin embargo, quedé cautiva de la antigua ternura.

—ALEJANDRA PIZARNIK

Contents

Foreword

Matthew Shenoda

Dulce, the sweetness: the sweetness of song, the sweetness of longing, the sweetness of corners whose edges have been rounded, the sweetness of an imagination open to the redefining of the present world. Like the birds that populate so many of his poems, Marcelo Hernandez Castillo's *Dulce* is a lesson in song, an instructive repetition of the melodies that shape the inner self. The poems here are for a reader willing to mix and remix, to reimagine themselves in a mirror sometimes true, sometimes convex, sometimes shattered in a thousand pieces. As he writes in his poem "Elegies".

These are the rules we were expected to follow:

Either praise the beautiful
or praise what is left over.

Choose the one that is most like a bridge.
Soak your hands and face in it.

And like a bridge, Hernandez Castillo finds a way to build words over several worlds: the world of a father and son, tender and rough; of a man and his lovers, imagined and real; over the borders of our limited empathies and concrete realities; between a nation and (un)nation, present and future; between all that swirls and eddies in the current around him as he continues to wade deeply in an effort to soak in his own words.

So often throughout *Dulce* we witness as Hernandez Castillo takes us through and back again. Like a muralist, collagist, or weaver, he loops and plaits, layers and reveals, creating a repetition that allows us to see each moment from multiple angles, to hear it again, to ravel and unravel like the bird's song in the first poem, "What You Can Know Is What You Have Made":

> The bird unraveled its song and became undone.
> > It couldn't figure out
> > its own puzzle in its mouth
> > so it gave up.

Unlike the bird, the poet does not abandon this puzzle but instead makes it the center of his aesthetic, using the weaving of the nest as a model for his lines: in and out, over and under, each thread revealed in myriad places. As he implicates himself, he implicates us and makes a new nation of his words. We, the readers, step back from it all, and we begin to see the arch of the poet's work, the definition of a future not yet known, the staking of a new space, a world imagined where the whole of a person can be considered, or as Hernandez Castillo writes in the last poem, "Cenzontle":

> Because the bird flew before
> > there was a word
> > for flight

> > > years from now
> > > there will be a name
> > > for what you and I are doing.

Of course this naming, this notion of the "new," has always been embedded in the architecture of the poet. As poets emerge and work to recast the language they sculpt, we make a place at the table for them to alter the poetic line and the language it carries in a manner all their own.

The art form expands and refines as a result of it. Marcelo Hernandez Castillo is no exception; he is a poet who has staked a rightful claim in a multitude of traditions and we eagerly embrace his *dulce*, his sweetness on the tongue, as we hold his words inside our mouths and give them breath as we read aloud. It is clear that we have embraced a poet of the "new," a significant voice for now and to come.

Acknowledgments

Grateful acknowledgment goes to the editors of the following publications, in which some of these poems first appeared, sometimes under slightly different titles: *Drunken Boat, Four Way Review, Gulf Coast: A Journal of Literature and Fine Arts, Huizache, Indiana Review, Luna Luna, Jubilat, Muzzle, Nepantla: A Journal for Queer Poets of Color, New England Review, The Offending Adam, The Paris American, RHINO,* and *Southern Humanities Review.*

"What You Can Know Is What You Have Made"

—Giambattista Vico

I want to say all of this is true
but we both know it isn't.
        The song becoming
        the bird becoming
        the song.
      Confetti for the newly fallen.

I am standing in a flower shop
to celebrate no one in particular.

What do I know of pleasure?

      It's not like pouring the sun into your hair—
      eyes glassy with milk.

      The bird unraveled its song and became undone.
          It couldn't figure out
          its own puzzle in its mouth
          so it gave up.

We already know what's at the other end of this.

The bird on the low branch
is trying to put itself back together.
If only it could hold still
long enough to open and close in my palm.

Everyone in the store is a widow
looking for her husband's face in the crowd.

The song
becoming the bird
becoming the song.

I want to run naked through the room pretending
that I am two lamps falling over.

What I know of pleasure I've learned only
while putting my clothes back on.

I open. I close.

I am always the obedient one.
    I want this to be easy.
And I can hear you already though you're not really here.
What's the point of any of this?

You say *open your mouth*,

so I do.
And, still, I wait.

Pulling the Moon

I've never made love to a man.
    I've never made love to a man but I imagine.

        I imagine pulling the moon.
        I imagine pulling the moon out of his brow.

Pulling the moon out of his brow and eating it.

        Eating and pulling his hair in silence.
A kind of silence when the moon goes out.

When the moon goes back and forth between us.

A kind of silence lit for a moment.
Seeing for a moment through the eyes of a horse.

        Through the eyes of the dead horse
        that burns slower than my hair.

My hair that burns the moon off.
My hair with a hand inside it.

Elegies

There are only masks
because we make them beautiful.

    The sparrow.
    The gold inside the sparrow.

Maybe I'm just looking for an exit.
Maybe the birds don't know it is not too late
to abandon their nests.

What if it was never the rain
promising our future?

    Yes, I loved you most in your big brown coat.

The room was too bright—
no one was afraid to die anymore.

        Serve the gin.

I loved the rain when it least resembled rain.
Kissing was sometimes like that—
    when it had nothing to do with our mouths.

Maybe I'm not trying hard enough.
If I'm tired then I'm tired.

The sick were hiding—
the robes were removed from the churches,
    more numinous than rain.

Yes, the light needs something to rest on.
Stay still.

Let me start over.
There was a mother.
> The sparrow was looking for an exit.
> Kissing was sometimes like that—
> looking for an exit.

The coattails dragged behind us.

Let me start over.
The cold was disguised as a mother's hands.

> The rain.
> The echo.

It was never a promise.

These are the rules we were expected to follow:

> Either praise the beautiful
> or praise what is left over.

Choose the one that is most like a bridge.
Soak your hands and face in it.

Gesture with Both Hands Tied

I'm going to open the borders of my hunger
and call it a parade.

But I'm lying if I said I was hungry.

If dying required practice,
I could give up the conditions for being alone.

I undress in the sun and stare at it
until I can stand its brightness no longer.

Why is it always noon in my head?

I'm going to run outside and whisper,
or hold a gun and say *bang*,

or hold a gun and not do anything at all.

The lamps that wait inside me say
*come, the gift is the practice,
the price is the door.*

Dulce

I will gather the voices of strangers mouthing my name.

> We are painting our names on each other—
> pushing our lungs
> to the other shores of our bones.

> If I could make honey I would feed you.
> I would lay prostrate before the thief broken in half—

> ribbons as the wound hurries to heal—

> *As large as my hand,*
> *as large as my mouth.*

We're never in much of a hurry.
It's easy to make honey from what is beautiful and what is not.

It is summer and I hardly know you.
What I do know is:

> 1.
> I will eat everything I love
> from its edge to its center.

> If it has an edge,
> if it has a center.

> 2.
> We make new friends then lose them.

3.
We never bake
another
goddamn pie again.

Either way it's a terrible future.
It's a movie where no one seems interested in the ending.

> I boil water on the stove for tea.
> I am alone in the house.

I think about the cock that's never been in my mouth
to shred this kind of quiet and piece it together again.

Wetback

After the first boy called me a wetback,
I opened his mouth and fed him a spoonful of honey.
  I like the way you say "honey," he said.

I made him a necklace out of the bees that have died in my house.

    How good it must have felt before the small village
    echoed its grief in his throat, before the sirens began ringing.

Perhaps we were on stage which meant it was a show,
which meant our only definition of a flower was also a flower.

I waved like they taught me,
like a mini miss something.

Yes, I could have ripped open his throat,
I could have blown him a kiss from the curtain.

  I wanted to dance by myself in a dark room
  filled with the wingless bodies of bees—

  to make of this our own Old Testament
with all the same beheaded kings
  pointing at all the same beheaded prophets.

  The same Christ running through every door
  like a man who's left his child in the car.

But the lights were too bright.
I couldn't hear him because I wasn't onstage.

I could have been anyone's idea of pity.

How quiet our prophets.
     Let my back remind him of every river.

Miel and *miel.*

          I pulled the bees off the string
          and cupped them in my palm.

I told him my Spanish name.

There was nothing dry on my body—
the lamps falling over in the dark of me.

El Frutero

Apá likes his fruit sweeter than his women.

I imagine Apá growing a garden
in his room next to mine.

I imagine Apá holding my mother's face
and slowly parting its earth for a plum orchard.

I know I'm supposed to look
away from his reaping.

My mother's face a blue
only known to exist in seeds.
Her limp body flapping with air.

I am young.
It is early.
She smiles at me and I don't look away—

her eyelids opening long enough
for me to see the ripeness
his hands are capable
of tending.

After he leaves, I will gently gather
the plums of her eyes
and tuck them
in my pocket and put her to sleep,

and bury them somewhere far,
so he will never find them.

I will rub salt all over my mother's body
so not a single blossom will ever grow there again.

I will feed every fruit down my father's throat
until he drowns of its sweetness.

Nuclear Fictions

We are completely miserable
but no one can tell
from the smiles on our faces.

Everyone is watching us on TV from home.
They think it's a show about foxes.

They know we know.
We bow to the image of their desire.

It's a game where the plastic is missing.
The world keeps coming
in and out of our coats.

A hummingbird
flushed in a cool electric drizzle.

There's always a man on the left
walking away from a woman.
There's always a woman on the right
walking away from a man.

Sometimes I can't tell if the cameras are on.
We nod our obedient heads.

Let them watch.
Let the sun sink to the surface of someone else's sky.

If we leave our bodies now,
they will find their way back to us.

Until then, touch me, I am gentle.
This has nothing to do with the rain.

Sugar

My father's hands split peaches in half and fed me.

Mouth / and nail.
　　Salt and / a little piss.

Always the leather, always / my ass bleeding with welts—
　　my ass purple with love,

Always / the belt he called Daisy.

And I said *hello Daisy,* / and she said *hello.*

And *he,* / bent over the sink with a bowl in his face,
and *he,* / the only tunnel of song for miles
　　in any direction.

The white belt—
Daisy and / *Daisy.*

And after it's over, we both know we have become men.
I love you, Daisy.

My father's hands will love a man / at the first sign of weakness.
　　Their suffering was our suffering.

They peeled the skin / off a lamb which was still breathing.
　　I remember its shrill cry,
　　but not the birria we made from it.

His hands were two doves / courting the lamb which was also a dove
　　in its thrashing.

14

They cut / through the air like ghosts.
They were large and capable / of great things.

    I always came / when they called.
        Ven, mijo.

    They always had peaches to put / in my mouth.

First Gesture in Reverse

He tenido muchos amores . . . pero el más hermoso fue mi amor por los espejos.

—ALEJANDRA PIZARNIK

I am lying on the floor
in a pair of panties.

Here I spread open
and become the knife
with its large smile
tilted away.

This is a star,
and this is a star.
I am thirsty.
It's called unbuckling.

I could be a bride.
Can you see it?
Aren't I a doll?

Here are my lips,
the rain, and the sound
they are capable of
inside each other.

Here the mirror
through which
I am unbearable.

The brown boy
waving the flag
of his father.
The brown boy
kissing the floor back.

If I can still close,
I will let the rain finish
what the light began
and never tell
anyone about it.

Immigration Interview with Jay Leno

What is your objective?
    To return all the children
    hidden behind the street lamps.

How long do you plan on staying here?
    I don't understand
    the question.

I said how long do you plan on staying here?
    We would have drowned
    even without our laughter.

Is that really your name?
    Yes, the clothes on the floor
    blossomed like the orchards in spring.

Have you been here before?
    There was a man who knew the way.
    I put his fingers in my mouth
    when he pointed in the direction of the sun.

So tell me, who are you wearing?
    The woman gave birth in the dark.
    I thought I felt hands where there were none.

    Everyone dug a useless hole.

Are you alone?
    North was whichever way
    the mannequins were pointing.

The softest bone was the one
that burned the longest.

Do you cry at night?
Are you alone right now?

Century of Good Metal

My skin is darker
than the flag burning
in the man's mouth.
Soy acampanado,
rezando por las entrañas.

Everything is larger
than the mothers robbed of grief.
Everything is to the left of them.

But who am I to the guns
painted for the young?

How large the paper kites
have grown over their faces,
as if the riddle
were meant to be answered.

Let this be the last time
a boy like me cuts himself open,

trying to find the swans
flapping their wings inside him.

Let this be the last time they appear.

And he will not move,
as if to say *I will not hurt you*,
afraid the smallest breath
will scare them away.

Immigration Interview with Don Francisco

In the church was the deepest
well of the city, where the priest
was lowered every morning.

[Please say more.   ]

I've split open the small fish
and counted the candles tucked inside—
all the pink nails tapping the wicks.

[Please elaborate.   ]

If I had children,
there would be no reason
to empty the bowls
stagnant with rain water—
no reason at all to keep saying
"you are almost."

[Please say more.   ]

The wasps: their multitude of clapping hands.

[Please elaborate.   ]

How small the dolls.
How insignificant
the hands that move them.

[Please say more.   ]

Perhaps the butterflies are mute because
no one would believe their terrible stories.

Rituals of Healing

Ramón, you were sick.

You weren't getting better,
but at least you were pretty.

Yes, the ticking nebula.
Yes, the machinery.

The sun performing
its ritual, swinging
its bare back across
the clockwork of sky.

You are wet and pretty.

I will believe in anything you do not
and bring it to you.

I will drink the blue night
gathered in your face
and weave your hair
for everyone watching you.

The edges of your body
touch everything
that isn't your body.

You are odorless.
Plastic even.

Your name is another word for fire.

What if we tell him
there's nothing wrong with him,
that he's only dying?

Origin of Prayer and Eden

At first no one knew what a man or a woman really was.

They had an idea.
There was a large ripple made by a small stone.

And that was that.

Instead everyone just swam in the river.
A wave and another wave behind it.

Eventually God too had to look away from himself.
We bowed our heads, not knowing to what—

> We hid paper hearts in a box with all of winter's
> beating wings inside.

Anything was holy
if we stared at it long enough.
How simple.

Hermosa.
Impossibility of union.

We pretended to be deer
pretending to play dead.

Gesture and Pursuit

I want to be the bride days later
when she is no longer a bride,
combing her hair in the mirror.

But it is too late.

I've already locked myself in a room
and imagined every variation
between witness and music.

I want everything to touch me
before it is bright enough
to slip through the house undetected—

like the sound of a child in the womb
tending its own window.

In which case anything is bright enough.

Is it too much to ask?
All I want is to run out of a church,
throw a bouquet,
and hop in a car
like my mother always wanted.

Drown

(after Brenda Hillman)

Yes, we drowned, then changed our minds,
      then drowned again,
      because we could,
because no one would know the difference—

      a leaf to its trembling
when it is no longer a leaf
but just a trembling.

      We splashed against the current—
a zipper of palms opening and closing.

We were too busy to notice
      that everything we touched
      was a little bell that was a little famous.

The sun opened its curfew and song

      as I swam to shake the sounds
of your laughter off me.

First Wedding Dance

The music stopped playing years ago
but we're still dancing.

There's your bright skirt scissoring
through the crowd—

our hips tipping the instruments over.

You open me up and walk inside
until you reach a river
where a child is washing her feet.

You aren't sure
if I am the child
or if I am the river.

Let's say the river is too deep
so you turn around and leave
the same way you entered—
spent and unwashed.

We are young,
our gowns are as long as the room.

I told you I always wanted a silk train.

We can both be the bride,
we can both empty our lover.

And there's nothing different about you—
about me—about any of this.
Only that you wish it still hurt, just once.

Like the belt your father whipped you with,
not to hurt you but just to make sure you remembered.

Like the cotton ball dipped in alcohol,
rubbed gently on your arm
moments before the doctor asks you to breathe.

Origin of Glass and Children

I want to believe this will end
with thousands watching
and throwing roses at us,
with lights and glitter in our hair.

But we both know how it ends—
we practice until we don't
need to tell our bodies how to do it.

In truth, we can't make anything happen between us.
Winter began inside—
no one knew,
but I knew.

Will you hold her to the light?
Will you breathe a little pink into her?
Not everything is a bright flute made of bone.

I'm convinced she is a swarm of honeybees.
What if they died not because they stung
but because they grew tired of stinging?

You wash the sand out of your hair,
where the mushrooms outnumber the stars.
We sit in the sun and quietly roll clay between our legs.

Winter begins with her hands
detached from the branches.

You knew,
you always knew.

Love Poem: A Nocturne

I split you from your child—

a bowl of water in one hand,

a small bell that doesn't ring
in the other.

I pour the water
over the bell and listen.

Half of you raptured in song,
the other half

a biography of grief
wholly unknown to me—
a sea of individual tremblings.

I've thought of naming her *Azucena*:
little wet bell.

I will keep her name in a jar
and wait for her to grow up and laugh
when I open the lid and tell her,
this is where you came from.

Please

My favorite pill is the pink and round one.

Lately I've been rowing toward the trees to see what they have left for me.

I could send you flowers but what's the point

if they will still be flowers when you get them?

If I'm lonely, put the bright birds back in their cages.

Love me as one priest confessing to another.

We dipped crisp cucumber slices into a bowl of yogurt.

Walking away was the only thing that made sense to me.

Rima

Rubi, we have lost so much time.

I am naked in the river.

Your eyes are larger than visible things.

We're broken the way things should be broken.

As Christ did, we did.
We knew how to touch.

Risen.

Our clothes are wet.

Don't you understand?
They will never dry.

Every blue center cut
out of every blue center.

Risen.

I can't tell you what other name to call it.

Consider the octopus.
If you had three hearts
would you really

want one to keep you alive
while the other two split you in half?

Rise.

Bi-Glyph

We made love then argued,
or argued then made love.
It didn't matter either way,
everything had the aftertaste of gasoline.

Even the floor.
Even your hair.

We were always reaching
into each other looking for something.

I'm lying if I said I didn't want this.

The light barely bright enough to tear
the languor from our bodies.

The rain outside had that thick

Midwestern glue to it.

I only wanted to look far enough back
to see where I split in half.

How dumb we were
endlessly searching
for a definite shape
our longing would take.

I leaned into you,
all of you,
as if in chorus.

Sing Once Found

You must sing to be found; when found, you must sing.

—LI-YOUNG LEE

Another doctor
pulled another child from you
and gave it to me.

He was gentle.
He was better than any knife.

Your one good dress
in my one good hand
in the only light.

We closed our eyes
and looked for each other.

The doctor was laughing,
and we were laughing,
and the babies were laughing.

We no longer remembered
in which direction to point
the living world
when it came
stumbling toward us.

We pressed our ears to the ground
and listened to the bells
in the throats of the dead.

Everyone thought they could hear
the sounds of children
when in fact

they all walked into a tree
and never came back out.

Miss Lonelyhearts

I don't know if we're doing this right,
as if *right* could exist between us.

We knew it would come to this—
    but we like it.

It's easy to imagine ourselves
    as loneliness tethered on a stick.

It's easy to imagine getting used to this.

    I pull my hair out one strand at a time—
        a relief at the end of my hunger.
    I wish I could be turned inside out again—
a deep purple that bone and fire make.

    There's nothing more that can be done between us.

            My teeth bite the carpet,
            your breasts on my back,
            your menstrual blood at its thickest,
            and the TV has been ranting
        on the same goddamn channel for three days.

I'm trying to convince you that I like it.

Tell me I'm pretty
and paint your name on my legs
with your lipstick so I can believe
it is my name and we both answer.

Tell me the story
where neither of us win.

Beat me the way our parents did.
Put your belt in my mouth. Call it *Daisy*.
I'm here, Daisy, hello.

I will eat it.
I will make it come back to life.
I promise.

We can live out the rest of our lives like this.
For now I will play the man, and you will play the woman.
Or you will play the man, and I will play the woman.
Or we will both play men, or we will both play women.

You will pull a child from between your legs that will not cut you.

But she will die, as they all have,
she will be still,
forever
only once in her life.

Cenzontle

Because the bird flew before
    there was a word
    for flight

        years from now
        there will be a name
      for what you and I are doing.

I licked the mango of the sun—

between its bone and its name
between its color and its weight,

      the night was heavier
      than the light it hushed.

Pockets of unsteady light.
    The bone—
    the seed
inside the bone—

      the echo
      and its echo
      and its shape.

Can you wash me without my body
coming apart in your hands?

    Call it *wound.*
    Call it *beginning.*

The bird's beak twisted
        into a small circle of awe.

        You called it *cutting apart*,
            I called it *song*.

Marcelo Hernandez Castillo is a poet, essayist, and translator born in Zacatecas, Mexico. He is also the author of *Cenzontle*, winner of the A. Poulin Jr. Poetry Prize, and *Children of the Land: A Hybrid Memoir* (forthcoming). He is a Canto Mundo Fellow and became the first undocumented student to enroll and graduate from the M.F.A program at the University of Michigan. As a founding member of the Undocu-poets campaign, which eliminated citizenship requirements from all first book prizes in the nation, he was awarded the Barnes and Noble "Writers for Writers" Award.